C000147705

About the Author

After leaving school, the author worked in the retail sector before deciding in her mid-thirties to go to university. After graduating, she trained to become a teacher and spent the rest of her working career teaching in Birmingham. Born in Wales, she spent most of her life living and working in the West Midlands where she lives with her partner, Philip. She loves travelling and has a holiday home in France. She also loves spending time in the great outdoors, whether it be running, walking, cycling or wild swimming.

TO

John,

Navigating Our Way Through Lockdown

Happy Birthday

love from

Rhanne
xx

Rhianne Colley

Navigating Our Way Through Lockdown

Olympia Publishers
London

www.olympiapublishers.com
OLYMPIA PAPERBACK EDITION

Copyright ©Rhianne Colley 2022

The right of Rhianne Colley to be identified as author of
this work has been asserted in accordance with sections 77 and 78
of the Copyright, Designs and Patents Act 1988.

All Rights Reserved

No reproduction, copy or transmission of this publication
may be made without written permission.
No paragraph of this publication may be reproduced,
copied or transmitted save with the written permission of the
publisher, or in accordance with the provisions
of the Copyright Act 1956 (as amended).

Any person who commits any unauthorised act in relation to
this publication may be liable to criminal
prosecution and civil claims for damage.

A CIP catalogue record for this title is
available from the British Library.

ISBN: 978-1-80074-459-2

First Published in 2022

Olympia Publishers
Tallis House
2 Tallis Street
London
EC4Y 0AB

Printed in Great Britain

Dedication

To my mum, Joan, and my partner, Philip, with love.

Introduction

The year 2020, what a year that was! It was the year the world was ravaged by COVID-19. I'm not a medical expert by any stretch of the imagination, but to put it in layman's terms, COVID-19 is a severe acute respiratory infection which for some people, particularly the elderly or those with underlying health conditions, can be fatal. At the time of writing, the disease is still with us and although there are now a number of vaccines available, we are still not out of the woods, although it's hoped things can get back to normal-ish, in the months ahead.

This potential deadly virus has impacted on everyone's lives in some shape or form; whether from the disease itself or the subsequent lockdowns (which were implemented as a way to slow down the spread of the virus) that were imposed on people in the UK and in countries around the world. For many, 2020 had a negative impact; there were of course the thousands of deaths and the knock-on effect for families dealing with the pain of bereavement. There were thousands of subsequent job losses and redundancies which impacted most severely on those working in hospitality and the entertainment industry. People dealing with depression, alcohol abuse, domestic violence, and the new phenomenon 'long COVID'. Oh yes, I nearly forgot, another negative impact; people panic buying toilet rolls and pasta! Such was the extent of this panic buying, the sale of these items had to be rationed, it sounds as though I made this up but believe me it really did happen.

For some people, myself included, in a perverse kind of way the lockdowns had a positive impact, and it brought out the best in people; more food banks sprang up, neighbours helped neighbours, communities came together, and at the beginning of the pandemic, much of the British public came together every Thursday evening to clap the NHS in recognition of the sterling work they were doing (and are continuing to do even now).

This journal takes you through how I, with my partner, Phil, tried to make the best of a bad situation, and how my quality of life, in my opinion has improved because of it. Lockdown has helped me bring into focus what's important in life and what isn't. During the lockdowns I used some of the skills I'd forgotten I had, such as sewing and cooking, and I've learned a few new skills along the way. Lockdown was also the perfect excuse to read more books (always a pleasure, never a chore) and I did that in spades. I'll state at this point that I know I'm one of the lucky ones and believe me I really do empathise with those less fortunate than myself and are suffering through no fault of their own.

The beginning

Over Christmas 2019 and well into the New Year, Phil and I were both really ill (we're convinced it was COVID-19, but at the time we had no idea it existed, and we thought it was just winter flu). Phil was much worse than me, in fact he felt so ill he had to see a doctor, something unheard of for him, as he would never normally go to see a doctor unless he absolutely had to. But despite feeling ill we made the best of it, we even managed to drag ourselves to the theatre on New Year's Eve to see a matinee performance of *The King and I*. It was an excellent performance, and Phil even managed to get through it without coughing every few minutes. Having said that, we were certainly glad to get back home at the end of the performance. Looking back and knowing what we know now, if we did have the virus, we could well have passed it on to other theatre goers and we most certainly wouldn't have gone had we known the risks.

In 2019 there had been much talk of climate change; there were TV programmes and articles written about plastic pollution in the oceans, and the damage fast fashion is doing to the environment. In light of this, I decided that my New Year resolution for 2020 would be to do something to help the environment. In the end, I resolved not to buy any more items of brand-new clothing (underwear and footwear not included I hasten to add) for the duration of 2020, and if I needed any clothes, I would either buy from charity shops or from that well-known auction site. However, little did I know when I made my New Year resolution, that I wouldn't be going anywhere to warrant wearing anything brand new! The holidays, the BBQ's, the birthday parties, the wedding celebrations etc., were all cancelled, it was literally a case of all dressed up, and nowhere to go.

Having said that, I did buy some clothes from that well known auction site, and I even managed to persuade Phil to use it when he needed some new jeans and like me, he's now a convert. I think the fact that he realised, he could get three pairs of pre-loved jeans for the price of one brand new pair might have had something to do with that.

The concept really made me think about what I need rather than what I want and moving forward I'll definitely think twice before buying brand new. Waiting for your parcel to arrive is also a bit of a thrill, and I love the different ways people pack their parcels. Most *sellers* use recycled packaging (as do I), an old carrier bag turned inside out or a used jiffy bag with a label stuck on the front to obliterate previous addresses. It really gives you a little insight into other people's lives. If I can, I make sure I re-use the packaging too, even if it does only end up as a pedal-bin liner.

At the time of writing, according to Clothes Aid, "350,000 tonnes, that's around £140 million worth of used but wearable clothing goes to landfill in the UK every year." It's a shocking fact and, in the past, I admit that I've been guilty of contributing to landfill through my impulse buys and fast fashion purchases, but I'll certainly try to minimise my throwaway attitude to clothing in the future. Another small thing we did to reduce our plastic use is to use soap instead of shower gel, and I've stopped buying conditioner. I know it doesn't sound much but doing something is better than doing nothing. I'm hardly using my car either, so at some point in the future I will evaluate whether or not I actually need one.

So, January rolled on, and by the end of the month we were finally feeling like our normal selves, so we went to Spain for a few days. It was a real pick-me-up, the temperature was in the mid-twenties, and it was lovely to feel the sun on our faces. We met up with friends, ate out and chilled out. We enjoyed it so much as soon as we got home, we booked flights to go again later in the year. By this point, although it was apparent the virus was running riot in China and other parts of Asia, there was still no real indication of what was waiting for Europe around the COVID-19 corner. Needless to say, that holiday in Spain was cancelled. Even though it was the airline that cancelled our flight, it took approximately four months to get a refund. The company kept trying to give us a voucher for use at a later date, but we held firm and waited it out.

February was also a relatively normal month for us (by that I mean we weren't unduly worried about the spread of the virus), we went to our holiday home in France for a few days over half term and celebrated St Valentine's Day with a meal in what could only be described as a very typical compact and bijou bistro. The food was delicious (as was the wine), and we were made to feel very welcome by the owner and his wife who came over and chatted to us in a mixture of English and French, which made quite an amusing conversation. We enjoyed the evening so much we promised ourselves we'd go back on our next visit.

It was also Phil's birthday in February (one of the very few people I know, who hasn't had to celebrate their birthday under some form of COVID-19 restriction), and we celebrated with a meal in a local restaurant, it was a great evening, the food and the service was excellent, and there was a really good atmosphere in the place. Little did we know that it was to be our last restaurant meal for some time, as by this time the virus was gaining a strong foothold in other parts of Western Europe, and it was inevitable that it would soon be making its way to the UK. In fact, I must check to see if the restaurant is still open, as it was one of the many restaurant chains in financial difficulties and they had planned to close some of their less profitable sites. I bought Phil a paddleboard for his birthday, but of course we were unable to use it for some time.

It was the end of February, and into March 2020 when things really started to change for the worse. The virus had killed thousands of people across the world, and it soon became apparent that the UK was not to be spared. In early March the first UK death from COVID-19 was announced and by mid-March, infections were widespread across the UK population. At this point most sporting events were cancelled, including the suspension of the Premier League, much to Phil's disappointment as he's a Wolverhampton Wanderers season ticket holder, and he didn't know how he'd cope without his football fix. Fortunately, he doesn't miss it as much as he thought he would.

It was obvious things were getting more serious when on 17th March 2020 NHS England announced that from the 15th of April 2020 all non-urgent operations in England were to be postponed in order to free up hospital beds for COVID-19 patients. By this point (as mentioned previously), lots of people had started to panic buy, and shops and supermarkets across the UK ran out of toilet rolls, hand sanitizer, soap, pasta, and other essential foodstuffs. Even flour and home baking products were nigh on impossible to purchase unless you bought online at inflated prices. Madness!

Eventually (far too late in my humble opinion), in a televised address, the UK Prime Minister announced that a UK-wide lockdown would come into force on 23rd March 2020. The British public were instructed to stay at home, except for limited purposes — shopping for basic necessities; for one form of exercise a day; for any medical need and to travel to and from work only when absolutely necessary. The overriding message was: 'Stay at home, save lives, save the NHS'. In essence every non-essential business was forced to close down! Businesses such as local shops, supermarkets, chemists, and shops selling essential goods were allowed to stay open. However, all sports and leisure facilities were forced to close, and even parks had to shut their gates (although the decision on parks was later overturned and they were allowed to partially re-open). Church services and weddings were banned, and even schools had to close to the majority of pupils. Only children of key workers and 'vulnerable' children were permitted to attend school.

The steps the government took weren't totally unexpected, as lots of other countries had gone into lockdown before us, so it was inevitable that the UK would follow suit. The first lockdown was in place until 4th July, but with some relaxation of the rules during May. For example, you could go out for exercise more than once a day, the parks were allowed to fully re-open, and we also saw the phased re-opening of non-essential shops and schools were allowed to open for pupils in Years 11 and 13. In the meantime, teachers continued to deliver lessons via the internet to those remaining pupils who were still unable to attend. When lockdown finally ended there was much joy and celebration across the country and when hairdressers were finally allowed to re-open, we both rushed to make an appointment!

Needless to say, the supermarkets were super busy over lockdown, and there were long queues outside, as the number of people allowed in at any one time was severely restricted. Getting a home delivery was like finding a needle in a haystack, but Phil persevered and, after hours spent hitting the refresh button, he managed to get us a fortnightly home delivery slot (which we still have, thank goodness).

Since then, there have been other restrictions and even another lockdown (although not quite on the scale as the first one). For me, the worst part of the lockdown (and the further restrictions that followed) was not being able to see my mum for weeks on end. Before the restrictions, I always visited my mum once a week, usually on a Thursday, and we'd go to a local café, where she lives in Stourport on Severn; we'd have a coffee, a toasted teacake and a good catch-up. We still e-mailed one another at least once a day and chatted on the telephone regularly, but it's not the same as seeing someone face to face. Fortunately, she has other family living nearby and my brother, Tony, does her shopping and goes to see her every day to make sure she's OK. My mum lived through WW2, so to her the inconvenience of the lockdowns is a walk-in-the-park; it beats being down an air-raid shelter by any stretch of the imagination.

Having taken early retirement from my teaching career twelve months prior to the first lockdown, I became used to having quite a bit of leisure time. I do a lot of walking and having been gifted a 'Fitbit' in 2016 I always do my best to get my 10,000 daily steps. I also run (when I say run it's more like a moderate jog) something I've been doing since 2004. I've since progressed to half marathon standard, and I've done about a dozen half marathons in total. However, this year all mass participation events including running events were cancelled. For me, that was probably a blessing in disguise, as I'd been having problems with my hip since 2018, and my running has had to be curtailed somewhat as a result of an annoying throbbing pain in my right hip. I started having physiotherapy, but my appointments have had to go from face to face to telephone consultations which is fine for me, but I can't imagine what it must be like for people who are waiting for cancer treatment or a hip replacement. The wait to get treatment must be both physically and mentally draining. Let's hope the NHS get back to normal as soon as possible, and people start to get the treatment they need when they need it.

Meanwhile, whilst I was enjoying life in the slow lane, Phil was still working one day a week in a school and spent the rest of the week working for himself. He set up his own company *Hooked on Physics* ten years ago, and until lockdown happened, he was very busy delivering hands-on interactive physics teaching training courses up and down the country and overseas. So as soon as lockdown happened, apart from his regular school income, literally overnight, like thousands of other company directors no doubt, the income generated through his company dried up! So much for the Prime Minister and the Chancellor 'putting their arms around everyone' as they promised they would; Phil is still waiting for those arms to go around him, as he has had no government support whatsoever!

The question was how could Phil possibly deliver face-to-face training courses, if all the schools were closed, and everyone had been told to stay at home? Not being one to sit on his hands, Phil did what Phil does and started to think outside the box. As a result of the school closures, teachers had to quickly adapt to teach online lessons and were using software packages such as *Google Meet* and *Microsoft Teams* to help facilitate this. Phil decided that using one of these packages would be all well and good, but he still wouldn't be able to get across to his delegates, how to engage students by using practical demonstrations in the classroom; something he does as part of his own teaching practice, and one of the fundamental principles of the courses he delivers.

A conversation with a colleague sparked off the idea of filming the experiments he'd used on the face-to-face courses, and luckily for him he had all the equipment he needed in our garage, and we had a mobile phone to film with of course! So, provided he could drum up enough interest that was the rough plan. Fortunately, his idea was well received by schools up and down the country, and he got plenty of bookings. I'm making this sound as though it happened at the click of a button, but I promise you it didn't. Phil was the brains behind the operation, and I was in charge of the filming. It took a lot of planning on Phil's part, he had to set up and demonstrate each of the experiments whilst simultaneously narrating. It was also very time-consuming and required us both to 'skill up'. However, having purchased and learned how to use lots of new gadgets and gizmos, we're both much more tech savvy now – but it was a steep learning curve. In the end, we filmed over one hundred different experiments, and this has enabled Phil to carry on delivering his teacher training courses and of course generate income. He's also delivering online lessons to school age students up and down the country.

The enforced spare time also gave Phil the opportunity to further develop his website www.hookedonphysics.com, which he had neglected somewhat due to lack of time, and to be honest lack of expertise. To get the website back up to speed, Phil called on the help of a website developer he knows, and between the two of them they've taken the website to another level! All those clips we filmed are now on his website, and schools can sign up to view them all for an annual subscription. Phil is still successfully delivering his material online and his website looks awesome. Well done, Phil, all your hard work paid off. In my opinion, there's not many people out there who could adapt to the situation Phil found himself in as quickly and successfully, and that's down to his creativity, problem solving skills, subject knowledge and sheer bloody-mindedness.

Gardeners' world

Fortunately, whilst on lockdown most of the UK was bathed in spring sunshine (April 2020 being the sunniest April on record for the UK). The warm, dry weather which started in late March was still continuing into early May, and I can vouch for that as I celebrated my birthday in the warm spring sunshine.

As spring is the sowing and growing season, Phil and I decided we'd try our luck growing our own vegetables. We already had an established apple tree and cherry tree and had grown vegetables in the past with limited success, but this time we really went for it. One of the first jobs Phil did was to make some planters for the back garden which, considering DIY is not one of his strengths, turned out remarkably well. Such was the success of the planters; he also made some trellis and more planters for the front garden. Feeling impressed with what he'd achieved, he bought lots of compost, seeds and plants, and we started down the path on our 'grow your own' journey (thank goodness the DIY shops were open throughout the lockdowns).

We tried our hand at growing, carrots, lettuce, peas, French beans, runner beans, courgette, spring onions, Spanish onions, beetroot, radishes, strawberries, tomatoes, and potatoes. As I alluded to previously, we'd had some success in previous years, and some things grew much better than others. Our successes funnily enough were the vegetables that we grew in compost; French beans, runner beans, Spanish onions (our best crop), tomatoes and lettuce. We used compost because our soil is really poor, we've tried enriching it with topsoil, but the soil is still poor, so any tips for soil enriching would be gratefully received. We also planted a plum tree and another apple tree, but we're yet to see how these develop.

We had limited success with our strawberries (it was a race to see who'd get the ripe strawberries first, the birds or us) and carrots, beetroot and radishes, but we completely failed with our courgettes and rhubarb so if anyone out there can give us some tips on how to grow courgettes and rhubarb, please let us know. At least in lockdown, the fact that you couldn't travel anywhere meant the fruit and veg was well tended. In the past we would have good intentions and plant things, then go on holiday only to find they were dead, or in need of some serious resuscitation when we arrived home again weeks later.

Another consequence of the mild spring was an abundance of cherries. Unfortunately, they weren't the big juicy black cherries that you can buy from farm shops and supermarkets, these were the very small *ornamental* variety. But what they lacked in size they made up for in number - there were literally hundreds of them and most (but not all) of them ended up on our drive! I was constantly sweeping them up and getting more and more frustrated. It seemed to me that it was cherries covering the driveway in the summer and then leaves in the autumn. I'd had enough and, in the end, I think Phil felt sorry for me, so he got someone to come and prune it. We used a tree surgeon, Anthony, who'd done work for us in the past. He's very good at what he does and, the tree is now about one third of its original size and, I'm pleased to report that I haven't had to sweep up any leaves this autumn.

As for the apples, they too grew in abundance. I gave lots away to family, friends, and neighbours, I made apple crumble and also cooked and froze some. Even after that there was a superabundance of apples left, so we wrapped the remaining apples in newspaper, put them into boxes and stored them on a shelf in our garage. A couple of weeks later, when Phil was in the garage, he said he'd heard a rustle and a scampering of feet. We couldn't work out why there would be an animal of any sort in the garage, as there was no source of food, but Phil had a light-bulb moment and remembered that we'd put the apples in there so the next day we went to inspect our hoard (or what was left of them by then). What a mess, the newspaper looked as though it had been through a shredder, and as for the apples, practically every apple had teeth marks gouged into them. What a waste of good produce! We placed the blame firmly at the feet of a squirrel who regularly visits our garden. We'd seen it earlier in the year nibbling away at the windfall apples at the bottom of the tree, and that was all the evidence we needed. Oh well, another learning curve; squirrel-proof your garage!

We're lucky that we have a bigger than average garden that backs onto a stretch of the Wyrley & Essington Canal. We used to go down to the canal bank and look at the ducks and swans from time to time, but we'd never really made the most of what was on our doorstep (or back garden in this instance). So, during lockdown we decided to give that part of the garden a makeover. We got rid of the garden waste that had accumulated, we gave the grass a good strim, and put down some new turf; we even put in a mooring point where we can tie up our kayak (more of the kayak later). We took a table and some chairs 'canal-side', and we got a lot of enjoyment out of it. We see a lot more of our neighbours as well, and we give them a wave or have a quick chat as they go along the tow path on the opposite side of the canal.

There have been a pair of mute swans on our stretch of the canal for a few years now, and they make their nest at the bottom of a neighbour's back garden a few metres from us. The female swan sat on the nest for what seemed like months on end, but it was worth the wait as she had five cygnets! I did some research and read that a female swan can lay up to ten eggs (which I thought was quite staggering)! We did see a family of seven cygnets earlier this year further along the canal near Pelsall, but that's the most I've ever seen. Our local cygnets grew really fast and were soon independent. They were a lovely sight to behold, but the adult swans would get very aggressive if anyone tried to pass the cygnets when they were sitting on the tow path. In fact, some days it was literally impossible to pass the swan family at all, and people would have to turn around and go back the way they came.

The cygnets are now nearly as big as their parents, although they're not as white in colour as they're still sporting lots of their brown plumage. At the time of writing four of the cygnets have left to make their own way in the world, and we miss seeing the whole family swimming majestically along. Our family of swans must be the most photographed in the local area; I know I've taken more photos and videos than you can shake a stick at, and the swans have been the subject matter for many of my Facebook posts. I also see people on the tow path photographing them, so it's not just me who has a swan obsession!

Along with the swans, there were also lots of ducks; moorhens, coots, and mallards, which meant there were lots of baby ducklings to keep us entertained. The water in our local canal is relatively clear compared to other canals and I wondered why this is so. Thanks to Robbie Cumming, I now have the answer (I came across one of his *YouTube* clips which provided me with an explanation). Apparently, it's because the water that feeds our canal is pumped from an old mineshaft fifty feet below ground and, because there is nothing getting into the water supply to contaminate it, it comes out clear. I think it must also be due in part to the lack of boat traffic on the canal over lockdown.

I love seeing the narrow boats go by, and we always give the narrow boaters a wave when we're at the bottom of the garden, even though the boats do leave a nasty trail of diesel in their wake. However, much worse than the diesel is the plastic pollution which you see on some stretches of the canal. Why do some people think it's OK to throw their rubbish in the canal or on the tow path? I think it's a disgrace, and those responsible should be ashamed of themselves. You always know when you're entering an urban area because that's when you start to see an accumulation of rubbish. Seeing all that pollution makes my blood boil!

We did think (and are still thinking) about buying a narrow boat, but what puts us off is the fact that the boats only travel at approximately 4 mph, and that we'd have to navigate twenty-one locks to get further afield than Wolverhampton City Centre. It's possible to avoid the twenty-one locks, if one heads in the direction of Birmingham, so the idea of the narrow boat is not completely dead in the water, so, watch this space.

On a positive note, the lack of pollution in terms of noise and air pollution over the first lockdown brought lots of birds to our garden, some of which had never paid us a visit before. The most unusual was a visit from a sparrowhawk. It was a real treat to see one in such close proximity, but by the time I'd reached for my iPhone to take a photograph, it had flown away. I also had the surprise of my life when I saw murmuration of starling's swoop onto the back lawn, for this event I'm glad to say I did manage to get photographic evidence. The sheer number of them and the noise they made was absolutely awesome, and it's something I certainly didn't expect to see in such close proximity and a pleasant change from the cooing pigeons and chattering magpies who are regular visitors and are more of a pest than a pleasure.

We've also seen other varieties of birds, whilst we've been out and about including herons, buzzards and a chaffinch, I'd love to see a kingfisher, but as yet I'm still waiting.

But it wasn't just here in the West Midlands where there were unusual animal sightings over lockdown. For example, a herd of around one hundred and twenty-two goats were spotted wandering around the streets of Llandudno nibbling hedges and eating flowers from people's gardens. It's thought, the lack of human activity in the town drew them down from their normal habitat. What a bizarre sight that must've been!

In 2019 we had a wooden structure built in the garden, similar to pergola but with a roof and two sides (so nothing like one really). The idea behind it was that it would provide shade from the sun in the summer, but it would also protect us from the wind on cooler days. It looked great and we had good use of it over the summer. So far so good you think, but then Phil decided that he'd like to be able to use it all year round. Once again, his brain went into over-drive and as always, he came up with a good solution. The idea was to have wooden doors on hinges so they could easily be removed if and when needed. The doors would give us protection from the weather in autumn and winter but could easily be removed for spring and summer. This was not something we could do ourselves, but we knew a man who could - our tree surgeon, Anthony! He did a fabulous job, just how we'd imagined it would look, and the *Garden Room* is now a wonderful space that we can use all year round.

We've made it nice and homely, and Phil even had the foresight to have a couple of electricity points put in. We now have a projector installed, so we can use it as a cinema room too. We even had a post lockdown sleepover with Phil's nieces and nephew - Phoebe, Libby, and Conor (aka, Jones PLC) and, on the rare occasions when there haven't been any lockdowns, or other forms of restrictions in place, we have used it regularly to entertain friends and family (whilst socially distancing of course ha-ha)!

We've even installed a butane wood burning type stove to keep us cosy and warm in the winter, and with our solar lights it's a really magical space. Phil has just finished making a bar that fits snugly in one of the corners. The framework for the bar is an old pallet that we had in the garage, and we had a lot of left-over wood from the *Garden Room* doors, so it was a real up-cycling project, if you're ever in the area and fancy a pint or a G&T, you know where to come! You never know it could be a future contender for the *'Shed of the Year'* competition or *'Amazing Spaces'*.

Oh, I nearly forgot, we also put a swing in the willow tree at the bottom of the garden. We lashed it onto one of the higher branches and although sometimes it swings a bit close to the tree trunk, it does what is says on the tin — it's a swing and it swings!

The great outdoors

I mentioned previously how much I enjoy walking, and for the last four years (thanks to my Fitbit) walking has become a part of my daily routine. Over lockdown walking took on a new dimension as we both did a lot more than we would do normally, and we also stumbled upon places we never even knew existed.

There's a stile about a three-minute walk away from where we live, and once you've climbed over the stile, you're on part of the 'Monarch's Way'. However, what I didn't realise (until I did some research) is that the 'Monarch's Way' is a 615-mile (990 km) route that traces the escape taken by King Charles II after he was defeated by Oliver Cromwell at the Battle of Worcester in 1651, and that the 'Monarch's Way' is the longest inland trail in England. Apropos of Charles II, there are a number of historical houses in the locality linked with his being in the area, Moseley Old Hall, Boscobel House, and the 12th century ruins of White Ladies Priory. Right, let's get back to the walk.

The first part of the walk takes you through the middle of farmland, then you cross a main road to continue along the path. Phil and I have walked this path many times before, but for some reason had never noticed the massive pool of water that sat shimmering in the sunlight. Apparently, the pool was a former sand and gravel quarry. We were gobsmacked, how could we not have known it was there? I wondered if it was a mirage but no, it was definitely there in all its glory, and there was plenty of bird life enjoying it too. We decided to go home a different way through 'Black Cat wood'. I'm not sure where the black cat was, but the wood made up for the cat's absence with a wonderful carpet of bluebells.

This became one of our regular walks in the spring and summer, we even did it on my birthday which is in early May. There is something magical about the wood when the bluebells are out. However, it's not so good when it's been pouring with rain as it gets very muddy. Even in bad weather I try to remember Alfred Wainwright's mantra from his book, *A Coast-to-Coast Walk*. "There's no such thing as bad weather, just unsuitable clothing." My advice would be; if it's muddy wear wellies, if it's cold wrap up warm, if it's raining take an umbrella and if it's snowing, go into the garden and make a snowman! We also did a lot of walking along various canal networks; however, we did so many there's a whole section dedicated to the canals.

A new experience for me in 2020 was open water swimming; something I'd wanted to do for some time. My inspiration came from the book *Waterlog* by Roger Deakin. He wrote so poetically and passionately about open water swimming that I knew it was something I wanted to try. The lockdown rules were relaxed in May 2020 to allow outdoor activities to recommence, so in order to realise my dream, I bought myself a pre-loved wetsuit, and I booked myself a swimming slot at Dosthill

Quarry which is just outside Tamworth. It's an amazing place, and as the name suggests it's a disused quarry which has been a centre for swimming since 1934. According to their website: "Not only have independent water tests confirmed the purity and clarity of the spring-fed lake, but also the presence of the spa mineral magnesium, considered to be the most important health mineral in the world". I was very lucky when I went the first time, as the water was quite warm, thanks to the lovely weather we'd had over the spring.

It was a very strange experience to start with, but I soon got used to it. The majority of people that swim there are what I would call 'proper swimmers', but I didn't let that put me off, and I just swam a few laps at my own pace. Every time I've been, there's been a heron either sitting on the branch of a tree or perching high up on the rocks, and it's probably wondering why there are people swimming around in his favourite fishing spot. Apparently, there's lots of different varieties of fish in the quarry so he'll no doubt be waiting for us swimmers to get out of the quarry so he can get on with his fishing.

Phil did swim with me once, but he says he finds swimming boring; he also likes to make sure that he can put his feet firmly on the ground should he need to, something which is impossible to do as the water is very deep in parts (it goes to a depth of 20m in the centre). So, whilst I'm enjoying my swim, Phil will go for a walk and take in the stunning scenery which surrounds the quarry. I really enjoy the tranquillity of swimming in the quarry and the connection with nature; it really helps to clear the mind. When I come out of the water, I feel relaxed and revitalised, and my skin feels lovely and soft. I would highly recommend it and it's not only me who endorses it; according to the Swim England Open Water website, there are a number of benefits to open water swimming which includes better sleep, better circulation, improved metabolism, increased happiness, boosted immune system and better skin. You can't argue with that, can you!

I noticed on the Dosthill Quarry website that they also offer moonlight swims, but I don't think I'll be signing up for that any time soon. The quarry is also used for diving, and for those of you who are of a certain age, you may remember the Milk Tray advert with the cliff diving scene; that scene was filmed at the quarry in the 1970s: "All because the lady loves Milk Tray". If you're interested, you can find the clip on the Dosthill Quarry website. There are also lots of weird and wonderful things at the bottom of the quarry too, including a shipping container and an old Land Rover; it's all on their website if you're interested.

Unfortunately, due to the COVID-19 restrictions the changing facilities are closed, so you have to change in the car park which can be a bit awkward. In order to save my modesty, Phil bought me a folding 'changing tent' to use when I came out of the water which was a good thing, because for those of you who've never worn a wetsuit, it's much easier to get into one than it is to get out of one. Having said that it's a bit of game getting the tent down and back into its bag; so much so Phil had to watch a *YouTube* clip to see how it's done!

As well as the open water swimming I've also got up close and personal to the water in my kayak. Having a kayak had never really been on my radar, but because of the lovely weather we had over lockdown we'd started to look into the cost of buying one with a view to taking it out on the canal. What I didn't expect however, was for Phil to buy me one as a 'thank you' gift for filming his physics experiments.

We weren't sure how often we'd use it, so we decided to look for a pre-loved one. We found some that we liked on an auction site, but we kept getting out-bid and due to supply and demand, the prices were astronomical (it seemed that we weren't the only ones who wanted a kayak). In the end we found just what we wanted on Facebook's *Market Place* page, a nine-foot fibre glass kayak. I emailed the seller, and it was still available, so we hot-footed it to Hanley Swan, Worcestershire, to collect it. Fortunately for us, Phil's car was large enough to accommodate it, although I had to sit in the back as it was a snug fit.

I'd never been in a kayak before, so it was a bit scary when later that same day Phil launched me from our back garden into the canal, but I soon got the hang of it, and I thoroughly enjoyed the experience. Phil also took a turn and we had great fun. The only problem was we were both soaked at the end, and there was a big puddle of water in the bottom of the kayak! We soon solved this problem by investing in a 'spray skirt' which is great for keeping the water out. We also invested in a life jacket and got a licence from British Canoeing, just to be on the safe side. I've used the kayak on numerous occasions, and I love paddling up and down the canal; it's a very different experience seeing things from a *duck's eye* view. The majority of people walking along the tow path are really friendly, they will give me a wave, and some will even stop to chat, and of course it's a great way to maintain social distancing.

The most awesome sight I've seen whilst out on the kayak was my encounter with a flock of Canada geese. I could see lots of Canada geese swimming along some way ahead of me, and at the same time a man happened to be walking along the tow path towards me, and I commented to him on the sheer number of geese, he said he'd counted at least sixty-five of them! Just at that moment, in unison, the geese started to flap their wings, and they flew out of the canal and landed noisily on the tow path. Once they were on the tow path, literally seconds later, (for some unknown reason), they all decided to fly back onto the canal. The cacophonous noise of them beating their wings and the splashing which turned the canal into a fountain for a few seconds was absolutely awesome, rarely have I seen such a wondrous sight. It is truly something I'll never forget, and I feel very privileged to have seen that spectacular event. I'm glad there was someone else with me who witnessed it otherwise I might have thought the whole thing was a dream! I'm still not particularly proficient on the water, but I enjoy it all the same, and I think that's what matters the most.

I mentioned earlier that I bought Phil a paddleboard for his birthday back in February, we could have taken this onto the canal, but we didn't fancy falling in the canal. So, for the time being it's still unloved and languishing in the loft. Hopefully, we'll be able to take it abroad with us next year, we can dream!

We've kept up our running, although we haven't done the miles that we did prior to COVID-19, when we'd normally be in training for one of the mass participations events such as a half marathon or a 10K. Over the festive period, we would have routinely taken part in either the local *Turkey Trot* or the *Pudding Run* but of course this year they have both had to be cancelled. However, we decided that we'd do our own version of the *Pudding Run*, we'll run on the same date for which it was scheduled, and run the same number of miles, and of course I'll wear my Santa hat. I'll have to make sure I buy some mini-Christmas puddings which we can award ourselves with at the end of the run, I've even got some old *Pudding Run* medals that I can re-cycle.

Like running, cycling was something I'd done prior to lockdown, but I've never cycled as much as I've done in 2020. The majority of my cycling was along the tow paths, but I also cycled to *The Well*, the food bank, where I volunteer a few hours each week, helping out with the administration. In September I signed up for the *Love to Ride Cycle September*, an initiative aimed at getting more people cycling. I set myself the goal of riding 100 miles in September, and I'm pleased to say I achieved my goal and actually rode 104 miles. I've just signed up for *Winter Warmers*, so let's see if I'm as enthusiastic riding in the winter as I was in September. Somehow, I doubt it!

As if that all that wasn't enough exercise, once the first lockdown finished Phil decided he'd join a local

Boot camp; according to collinsdictionary.com, "A boot camp is a set of intensive exercises done on a regular basis and designed to improve strength fitness" and that's why I didn't go with him. It's the word 'intensive' that puts me off, I don't mind a bit of gentle exercise, but intensive, no thanks that's not for me.

The boot campers met in a field close to where we live, and there, they were really put through their paces! They were out in all weathers too; sun, rain, wind, cloud and sometimes a combination of all four elements! And the mud - that was the worst. There were many occasions when Phil came home soaking wet and caked in mud, rather him than me.

In conclusion, my advice to anyone would be; if you can get into the great outdoors, go for it; there's something for everyone it's great for your physical and mental health, and it doesn't have to cost you a penny.

Who needs the canals of Venice?

As you have probably gathered by now, Phil and I have developed an obsession for walking, and our favourite walks must be the ones along the canal network. We've had great fun exploring them on foot, on our bikes, in the kayak, and if we go further afield, we'll drive to a certain point and start the walk from there.

Our local canal, the Wyrley & Essington was built in the 1790s after an Act of Parliament authorised a canal to be built from Wolverhampton to the coal mines at Wyrley Bank. It is also known locally as the Curly Wyrley because it follows the contours of the land, and as such there was no need to build locks, which of course at the time would have been difficult and expensive to build. However, water supply was a constant problem, so the canal had to be extended to the reservoir at Chasewater (constructed in 1797) for the express purpose of supplying water to the canal. Another water source which helps maintain the level of water is the disused mineshaft at Bradley.

We've explored the length and breadth of our local canal network, all seventeen miles of it. Some of it we've explored on foot, but we've also been farther afield on our bikes. It's lovely to cycle along the tow path, there's no traffic (apart from walkers and other cyclists) or pollution (apart from the rubbish spots), and again it's a chance to connect with nature and breathe in the fresh air. We've even taken a little detour onto the little-known Cannock Extension line, which is 1.5-mile diversion off the Curly Wyrley. It's not a particularly pretty stretch, but interesting enough as it has a few of the old arched, brick-built accommodation bridges. There's a lot of these old bridges along the various stretches of the canals, but around the Black Country you'll also see many old iron bridges because of course the Black Country was a producer and manufacturer of iron and steel. There's a lovely nature reserve at Pelsall, and we often sit on a bench enjoying the peace and quiet. I have recently learned that it wasn't always that way, as back in the 1800s there used to be at least three collieries and a pumping station there, hard to imagine now!

We've also cycled South from Wolverhampton along the Staffordshire & Worcestershire canal to Wombourne and back, which was a 26-mile round trip. I managed to fall off my bike twice on that occasion, but no harm done to the bike (or me), it was just my pride that was hurt. We've also walked the stretch from Bratch Locks to Swindon. Bratch Locks is a really interesting place noted for its industrial heritage and, apart from the locks themselves, there's the very pretty Bratch pumping station; built in 1895 in a Gothic style (it's often described as a fairy-tale castle). It was originally built to supply the water for Bilston (now a suburb of Wolverhampton). After falling into disrepair in the 1960s, it's been brought back to its former glory and is now Grade II listed. There are some pretty toll houses on the Staffs & Worcs, but they a look as though they haven't changed since they were built, and in my opinion, are in need of some restoration. Once you're past Bratch Locks and Wombourne it all gets a bit industrial and noisy, but once you get nearer to Swindon Locks it becomes easier on the eye (and ears). If you were to continue South, you would end up in Stourport on Severn where the canal meets the River Severn, which in turn meets the Bristol Channel.

On another occasion we decided to leave the canal and make our return journey by road (as it's a lot quicker than cycling along the canal). Coming back, Phil spotted a road sign for the Wyrley and Essington Nature Reserve, something else we didn't know existed! We didn't stop on that occasion, but we did go back some weeks later and got the surprise of our lives when we found ourselves walking along a dis-used section of the canal, which is known as the *Lord's Hayes Branch*, so called because it was Mr Lord who owned the *Hayes* or hedged area on which that particular stretch of the canal was built. It was abandoned in 1930 and filled in under an 'Act' in 1954. It's fascinating, very overgrown and the canal bed has all but dried up in places. There's an old accommodation bridge called Bakers Bridge, which would have given the farmer access to his fields on either side of the canal. The canal looks almost prehistoric; lots of trees have fallen into the dried-up canal bed and there are long plant tendrils hanging from the bridge, which you have to part with your hands to get through. We ran along it the following weekend just to see where it finished, and much to our surprise, it finishes near Sneyd Junction, which is only a couple of miles from where we live.

On another occasion when out cycling, we left the canal and came home via a village called Shareshill. Phil was ahead as usual, when suddenly he made a left turn, I too made the turn but a little too sharply, and both the bike and I went flying across the gravel. I didn't want to damage my bike, and I somehow managed to get my body underneath it as best as I could. The reason Phil had made the turn was to look at the village Church of St Mary & St Luke. He was so interested in the Church; he didn't even notice I'd fallen off my bike. I was a lot more battered and bruised than my last fall but again, no bones broken… just my pride!

The Church is most unusual; it's a mix of Medieval and Georgian styles, and it even has a balustraded parapet (which basically means a balcony). There are musket ball scars on the tower from the days of the Civil War and sharpening marks, which are attributed to men sharpening their arrow heads on the walls; all that history in one little Church! Unfortunately, lockdown meant that it was locked, so we couldn't see the interior. We'll have to go back post COVID-19 and have a good look inside.

Outside the church there was a plant sale with an honesty box, somewhere to put the money for any purchases made. We liked the look of some of the herbs but didn't have any money with us (or anywhere to put the herbs), so we agreed to come back in the car the next day with some money. The next day saw us back at the Church, we chose and paid for our herbs and, as the weather was good, we decided to go for a walk around the village. It's a very nice village with the aforementioned Church, a community shop, post office and a pub, but what we didn't expect to see was an alpaca farm! I had been up close and personal to alpacas three years previously because Phil had bought me a voucher for an alpaca experience.

The experience involved my choosing an alpaca; feeding and grooming it and then taking it for a walk (I say 'it' as I can't remember whether male or female). They're strange creatures, but I didn't dislike them; their wool is very soft and, thankfully mine was very tame. There was also a llama amongst the alpacas, and I'm glad I didn't choose that one, as it was lively to say the least, and a real 'attention seeker'. At one point the llama's lead got entangled with mine and, myself and the llama's walker (and our respective animals) ended up in a right tangle; you could have called it a llama drama, and it was most amusing, particularly I'm sure to those watching from the side-lines! Seeing the alpaca farm in Shareshill with all those cute creatures was a lovely surprise and brought back lots of happy memories.

We've also been North along the Shropshire & Union Canal as far as Wheaton Aston. Part of this section takes you over an aqueduct, which was built by the famous industrialist Sir Thomas Telford in 1832, it's a real feat of engineering. The stretch to Wheaton Aston is very different to our local canal in that it was cut through an embankment. It's very high on both sides of the canal and it seems strange not to be able to see any of the land around you but having said that Phil's decided that it's now one of his favourite stretches of canal. There's a lovely pub on the canal bank at Wheaton Aston, but unfortunately when we did our walk, we were in the second lockdown and the pub was closed. What we did see on that day, however, was something I didn't expect to see in the 21st Century; a coal barge which was actually doing what it was built to do i.e., deliver coal. I even heard one narrow boater shouting to a neighbour, "Don't forget the coal barge is coming today". Being November, the *liveaboards* were obviously stocking up with coal for the Winter. The whole thing was very surreal, in fact, I felt as though I was an extra in a Charles Dicken's film.

If it hadn't been for the lockdowns, I don't think we would have had the pleasure of any of these sights. It's been wonderful to have seen so much beautiful countryside and, there's so much more to explore. In fact, there's over 2,000 miles of canals and rivers in England & Wales.

I've recently joined the Canals & Rivers UK Facebook page where people (including me) share photographs of their canal and river walks. There's over 21k members in the group, so you see it's not just me who's got the canal bug. In fact, one of the first pictures I uploaded received close to five hundred *likes* which I found quite astonishing! I'd better own up at this point and say that it was Phil who actually took the photograph; I just uploaded it to the Facebook page. The Facebook page has also been informative as it has even taught me how to 'sex a swan'! I uploaded some photographs of our local swans and admitted not knowing which one was male and which one was female. Someone from the group sent me a message to say that it's all to do with the size of the swan's proboscis (in the swan's case this is the black bump on the beak). If it's a large bump, it's likely to be a male swan (cob), and if the bump is relatively small the swan is likely to be female (pen). Another person advised that you can also tell the sex of a swan by the size of the neck, the swan with the wider neck is likely to be male. I don't think this is an exact science, but any knowledge is better than none.

Practically every time we go along the canals, we see a heron somewhere along the way. They are very majestic birds, but not a favourite in our family as a heron ate most of my Mum's goldfish. It only left two, and I think there were ten in the pond at the time. The pond has since been replenished with fish and it's been heron proofed (we hope). Apparently, it's very rare for a heron to eat fish from a garden pond so it must have been very hungry to do so. I still like seeing them but don't tell my Mum! Apart from the herons and the occasional fox, we haven't seen much other wildlife. However, our friend Lisa, who also likes walking along the canals, has seen a couple of otters and we met a bird watcher who'd seen a kingfisher. I'm sure the wildlife is out there, perhaps we don't look hard enough!

It's strange to think that over 200 years ago the canals would have been busy with barges and narrow boats transporting goods up and down the country. The water would have been heavily polluted as would the air because of the smoke billowing out of the factory chimneys; I don't expect there would have been any fish or other wildlife either. The railway boom of the 1840s was the death knell for the canals, and over time they became redundant. We are fortunate that someone, somewhere back in the late 1960s had the foresight to restore them so we can all enjoy them for living, for leisure and for pleasure.

You really don't know what's on your doorstep until you step outside and start exploring, and best of all, the canals are absolutely free! We're not done yet as there are many more tow paths out there waiting to be explored.

Apropos of canals, we have two lovely prints hanging in our house by a local artist called Paul Horton. The prints depict different Victorian industrial scenes, and would you believe it, both feature a canal!

Baking & other types of making

Before the lockdown, I'll be honest I didn't spend a lot of time in the kitchen. It was a room in which I didn't linger for any length of time! I knew how to cook and did a bit of baking, but it was born out of necessity rather than being something from which I actually got any pleasure from. But I'm pleased to say those days are gone, and I'm now a born-again baker and homemaker. Having said that, I always made sure I had a few basic ingredients in my kitchen cupboard, enough to rustle up a batch of fairy cakes, if I felt inclined. I mention this because if I hadn't had any ingredients in the cupboard, I wouldn't have been making anything, as shops and supermarkets quickly sold out of home baking ingredients as demand definitely out-stripped supply. You couldn't buy caster sugar or any type of flour; bread flour was like gold dust, even cake mixes, and baking cases were sold out. The lockdown certainly put home baking firmly back in fashion.

I think the first thing I tried my hand at over lockdown was a loaf of bread. Ambitious I hear you cry, but don't worry I dusted off the bread maker (literally) and with some strong bread flour which was well past its sell by date and some dried yeast I found at the back of the cupboard I set to work. The end result wasn't as good as I would have liked, but I wasn't too disappointed. It was definitely edible, and I vowed to make more as soon as I could get my hands on some bread flour.

I did manage to get some eventually, but it wasn't easy. As I said, all the supermarkets had sold out, so I had to buy online, but that was also difficult, and the only way I could get hold of any was to buy in bulk. I have made a couple of loaves since, and they have turned out really well (maybe because the flour was in date this time). A positive thing that came out the explosion in home-baking was how sales increased for the traditional flour mills, and they had long waiting-lists for customers wanting to buy flour. Let's hope the trend of buying flour from traditional mills continues when the pandemic is finally over.

Our favourite meal when we go to Spain is paella, so Phil decided that he'd make me a paella for my birthday (I made it in the end but that's another story). The ingredients were delivered as part of our online order, including a sachet of spices to add to the rice, and I'm pleased to say it was a real triumph and again it's something we've done a few times since. I think I'd rather be eating a paella in Spain with blue sky, sparking sunshine and a breath-taking view of the sea, but it looks like that wish will have to wait a while longer.

Earlier in my journal I told you about the abundance of cherries we had over the summer. We did eat some of them (not many as they were rather small), but what to do with the rest? I borrowed my Mum's ice-cream maker, and I tried my hand at making cherry ice-cream. It was rather fiddly removing the stones from the cherries, but it was well worth the effort. The recipe I chose was very decadent as it included a lot of fresh cream, but it was extremely good and worth all those extra calories! I also mentioned that we had grown beetroot. Although they weren't as big as we had hoped there was plenty of them. Again, what to do with the surplus? I looked up some recipes online, and in the end, I plumped for a beetroot cake, something I never thought I'd make. Like the cherry ice-cream, it was a bit fiddly and even messier than de-stoning the cherries. Once you'd peeled the beetroots, you then had to grate them. Fortunately, I knew it would be a messy job, so I made sure I was prepared. However, it was well worth the effort as it was delicious. The taste is hard to describe, but I'll try. I'd sum it up by saying it tasted 'earthy', not as sweet as carrot cake but similar in terms of texture. It would have been better with some cream cheese icing, but I wanted to see what it tasted like unadorned! It got a double thumps-up from everyone who tasted it, and it's something I'll try again. I told my friend, who has a café just outside Brighton about it, and she said they make chocolate and beetroot cake which sounds amazing, so that's something I might try next year.

Our canal walks in the late summer/early autumn found us foraging for blackberries, and thanks to the spell of warm weather earlier in the year, the blackberry bushes were dripping with fruit, and every time we went for a walk, we made sure we took a plastic tub with us and picked until our tub was full. I thought I'd try my hand at jam making, something which I felt a bit nervous about as I was worried that the jam might not set.

However, there was no reason to worry as unbeknown to me at the time, blackberry jam is the easiest jam to make as blackberries contain a high level of natural pectin (a chemical which helps the jam to set), so it was literally a piece of cake, or should I say a jar of jam. It was a great success and I wish I had made more. It's something I'll definitely do again next year. In fact, we've talked about jam making on a bigger scale. Foraging for fruits is fun and free, so the only cost would be that of the sugar, and we've started saving empty jam jars so you never know, we might have a market stall selling our homemade blackberry jam.

Over lockdown my Mum cleaned out her kitchen cupboards and passed me some baking tins she no longer wanted, including a muffin tin and a griddle. I did try out a batch of blueberry muffins, but they didn't taste as good as the ones you can buy from the supermarket, but I might have another go one day. As for the griddle, with my being Welsh, there was only one thing I could possibly cook on the griddle and that was Welsh cakes. My Nana used to make lovely Welsh cakes as did one of my Great Aunts, but after they died it seemed as though the Welsh cakes died with them. Until, that is, Phil and I went to Cardiff back in October 2019.

I was taking part in the Cardiff half Marathon, and Phil was there to support me. He waved me off at the start and then unbeknown to me (because of course I was in the process of running 13.1 miles), he went to the 'Fabulous Welsh cakes' shop in the Castle Arcade and bought a batch of Welsh cakes. They were just what I needed when I finished the half marathon (where incidentally, I ran a personal best time of 1hr 59mins & 45secs) and I vowed at that point that I'd have a go at making them myself. However, that vow went onto the back burner, that is until lockdown and the gifting of the griddle!

The Welsh cakes that Phil bought were a mixture of traditional Welsh cakes and other flavours; chocolate chip and lemon (not together), if my memory serves me well! For tradition's sake, I made my first batch with my mum, and we were very pleased with the results, so much so that they didn't last very long. I've made them a couple of times since but I'm still not getting the temperature of griddle quite right, but practise makes perfect, and I'm happy to carry on practising until I get it right (although I'm sure they'll never be as good as my Nana's).

Such was my kitchen confidence I decided I would make my own Christmas cake, another first (although I've seen my mum make enough Christmas cakes over the years, so I had a rough idea what to do). I managed to get all the ingredients I needed, and I think I did a decent job. I fed the cake regularly with a good slug of whiskey, which must have helped. But the proof of the pudding (or cake in this case) is in the eating. Making the cake was the easy part because as December drew nearer, I knew the day would come when I'd need to put the marzipan and icing on. I will admit at this point that I bought roll-on marzipan and icing, maybe I'll make those myself next year (or maybe not)! I have since put the marzipan and icing on the cake, and I must admit it was much easier than I thought it would be (although I did watch a couple of *YouTubes* clips beforehand which helped). My enthusiasm for baking must have been evident, as I had quite a few *kitchenalia* gifts for Christmas!

My mum is a very competent dressmaker, and when we were youngsters, she made most of our clothes. I still remember some of the clothes she made for me, and these are the ones that stand out the most; a yellow (Mum seems to think it was pink) cotton top with an elephant embroidered onto the front, a pink flowery dress with rows of smocking at the top, but one of my favourites was a black PVC pinafore dress (I really loved that pinafore dress) and, she even made my first Holy Communion dress. Some of Mum's sewing skills must have rubbed off on me as I'm not a bad sewer myself. I recently found out when chatting to Mum about our sewing prowess, that my Great Grandmother, my mum's paternal grandmother was a tailoress; so, sewing is definitely in the genes. But my poor sewing machine has been left languishing for a good many years, as I've been too busy doing something else, but I'm pleased to say it's back out now and has been put to good use. I had actually forgotten what a good machine it is. It does literally everything apart from make the tea (OK I'm exaggerating here).

Mum has one of those lovely old Singer sewing machines, which was given to her by her parents for her sixteenth birthday, (she was eighty-six in 2020 so you do the math) but unfortunately, it has seen better days and needs a bit of TLC. I did e-mail *The Repair Shop* to see if they would restore it for her, but I suppose these old machines are a bit commonplace, and we didn't hear anything back from them. But if there's anybody else out there that's up for the job, please get in touch.

One of my first sewing projects over lockdown was to make bunting for the *Garden Room*. At this point the *Garden Room* looked bare, so I decided to give it a makeover in the form of bunting. I rooted out a stash of fabric that I had squirreled away in the loft and set to work. It was a real mishmash of fabrics that I had to choose from, but I don't think that matters when it comes to making bunting. Even though it got a bit tedious, I was pleased with the end result and the bunting is still hanging in there (literally).

My next project was to make face coverings (I never thought I'd be writing that as part of a sentence never mind actually have made the things). At the onset of the pandemic, there was a lot of debate about the benefits of wearing a face covering in order to help limit the spread of the virus. However, on 4th March 2020, Professor Whitty, the government's chief scientific advisor said that "Wearing a mask if you don't have an infection reduces the risk almost not at all." And on 6th March 2020, the World Health Organisation endorsed this. However, at about the same time, in other European countries the wearing of face coverings was seen to be beneficial, and the wearing of face coverings in indoor public spaces became mandatory.

Phil and I had visited China a few years previously and noticed at the time that the majority of the population wore a face covering. This was in part because of the high levels of pollution in the cities. However, to my way of thinking if it helped reduce the amount of pollution ingested, surely it would also help prevent the spread of disease. In light of this sometime in March 2020, I set too and started my face covering production line! I made a couple for myself and a couple for Phil (in the Wolves *Old Gold* colours of course). My mum also thought they were a good idea, so I made some for her. My mum is a bit more discerning than me however and wanted her face coverings in a variety of different colours, so they'd go with her outfits and of course I obliged. Such is the popularity of wearing a face covering there's even designer face coverings now!

I was way ahead of the curve making my face-coverings as it wasn't until June 2020 that they became mandatory on public transport in England. Then we had to wait until July 2020 until the government announced that the wearing of face coverings in shops in England would also become mandatory. As ever the UK government was way behind other European countries with the compulsory wearing of face coverings, and they were forced to make yet another U-turn, one of twelve at the last count, but I'm sure it won't be the last one!

For my birthday, my sister, Mary, gave me a quilting kit, which I thought was nice, but I'd never done any quilting, and it all looked a bit daunting, so I put it in the drawer, out of sight, out of mind! However, I thought that if I don't try to do it when I've got lots of spare time, I'd never do it, so I got it back out of the drawer and got started.

It's an American quilting kit (apparently, they're really big on quilts in the US) and it's a 'Log Cabin' design. The kit was enough to make twelve log cabin blocks (each block when finished measured about 9.5" square) and each block contained twelve pieces of different sized fabric which had to be sewn together. I can feel you nodding off at this point, that's exactly how I felt, and it took me many hours to put it all together; good job we were in lockdown because it is one of the most time-consuming things I have ever done in my whole life!

Having made the twelve blocks, I wasn't sure what to do with them all. In the end, I decided to make three cushion covers made up of four blocks per cover. Now to the actual quilting part - the next step was to sew the four squares together to make one big square, then you have to add a layer of 'batting' (technical term for cotton type backing fabric) to the back of your big square, and then stitch over both layers in order to create a quilted effect. Once I'd done that, I had to find some fabric to make up the back of the cushion, and then sew that to the quilted square to create my cushion cover.

The first two cushion covers I made were for myself, but the final one was for a Christmas present, so I needed to raise my game. Instead of doing the back of the cover in one piece of fabric, I decided to use an envelope design for the final one. Using my good friend *YouTube*, I looked at a number of tutorials on envelope backed cushion covers and had a go myself. It was a lot easier than I imagined it to be, and I wished I had made the effort with the first two. However, I've got to say, the easiest part of the whole process was stuffing the cushions into the covers. I'm very pleased with my cushions, but would I do quilting again, definitely not.

At least I've tried it, and as a result of my efforts I've got three unique handmade cushion covers.

I also made a blouse, which I was very pleased with, but obviously I'm still waiting to go somewhere nice to wear it. I did think about making a matching face covering but decided that might be a bit over the top!

Along with sewing I've also found my 'crafty' side, and I did a lot of Christmas crafting; I made a Christmas wreath and some Christmas mice to hang on the Christmas tree (don't try this at home, each mouse takes hours and hours to complete, and to be honest they're not worth the effort, much like the quilting). In the end we bought a tree in a pot which lived outdoors on the patio, so the paper mice didn't get used in the end. Maybe I'll use them as Christmas gift tags!

A good book

I'm going to put it out there — I love reading; I read at home, I read on holiday, I just love to read, but I didn't really start reading books by *proper authors* until I was in my early thirties, prior to that I was an avid reader of the *chick lit* genre. My more serious reading coincided with my going to university as a mature student. I suppose I felt that being 'well read' was synonymous with attending university and, my journey as a 'serious' reader began and, what better place to begin my journey than with Charles Dickens.

The Pickwick Papers was the start of that journey, and it was that book which got me hooked. I fell in love with *The Pickwickian* characters, and the joviality and wit held within those pages; and to think Charles Dickens was only twenty-four years of age when he wrote it back in 1836. Over the ensuing years, I went on to read the popular Dickens' novels although I have to admit some of his books were more enjoyable than others! I even dabbled with Dostoevsky but found his books a bit grim (unlike the brothers Grimm)!

Another of my favourite books is Jerome K. Jerome's *Three Men in a Boat,* for me it's one of those 'laugh out loud' books, and it too has fantastic characterisation in the form of those three men in a boat, not forgetting my favourite four-legged member of the team; the mischievous Montmorency "…whose ambition in life is to get in the way". I also read his later book *Three Men on the Bummel*, but I didn't find it as funny; maybe I should give it another go? My Dad was an avid reader and would often have about three different books on the go. He also loved *Three Men in a Boat* and found it as funny as I did. He was really pleased when I started reading the *Classics* and would often jokingly comment that he was so glad he'd taught me to read! Mum can recall many occasions when Dad would go upstairs to read one of us a bedtime story and, sometime later she would come upstairs to find he had fallen asleep. My brother, John, works at a secondary school where he is head of English, so a love of literature must run in the family.

I'm a big supporter of the library service and, until March 2020, I was a regular at my local library. I loved browsing the shelves looking for some little gem that I knew must be there waiting for me and, of course the library is probably one of the earliest examples of re-cycling; so, what's not to love about the library? Luckily, I have a *Kindle* so the library closures meant I could still get my reading fix. Apart from the cost of some books (which to my mind is astronomical), reading from a *Kindle* is just not the same as having a physical book in your hand. A *Kindle* is convenient and lightweight, you don't have to get them back to the library on time and of course you can change the font size (great for someone like me who has to wear reading glasses), but for me, they're just not the same.

There's something about holding a book and turning the pages; I like looking at the cover picture, reading the blurb and the information about the author and you just can't get that same feeling with a *Kindle* (that's my opinion of course). I'm grateful that I have it but, since I found out about my library's click and collect service, which they launched at the back end of the summer, my *Kindle* has been put onto the subs bench! When I first heard about the click and collect service, I got very excited. The thought of being able to hold a real book again was so good. To access the online service, I needed to have a log-in and a password. and as with most things technical, this was not the easiest of things to set up. However, once I'd overcome that obstacle the world of *tangible* books was at my feet.

Having chosen and reserved my books online, I couldn't wait for the telephone call to tell me they were ready for collection. I received the telephone call only to be told I would have to wait seventy-two hours before they would be available for collection. Talk about someone bursting my bubble, seventy-two hours felt like a lifetime! The reason for the delay is that, once the books have been selected, they have to go into quarantine (I'm not making this up by the way). At the start of the pandemic, it was thought that traces of the virus could stay on hard surfaces for up to 2–3 days and on paper/cardboard for anything up to twenty-four hours. It may sound a bit excessive, but always better to be safe than sorry I suppose. Having the click and collect service was a real lifeline to me, as I'm sure it was to many others, particularly those living alone.

My local library has a covid-safe system for returning books. All book returns are to be left in a large brown wheely bin, which is secured to a post outside the library with something akin to a bicycle chain. On one occasion, I put my books in the bin and my face covering fell in too. Mine being the only books in the bin at that time meant they'd gone straight to the bottom, as had my face-covering! I did say it was a large bin, in fact it was nearly as tall as me (or as small as me, as I'm only 5'3"). I tried to reach in to retrieve my face covering, but my arm wasn't long enough. I then tried to tip the bin a bit, but it was attached to the post so that didn't work either. Fortunately for me the library wasn't open at this point, as I'd arrived early. I looked at the fastening which was holding the bin to the post and decided that if I could untangle it a bit, I'd be able to turn the bin onto its side. This was easier said than done, but I did manage to lower it enough to retrieve my face covering. However, it was at this point the librarian opened the doors and, I felt mortified that I'd been caught rummaging in their bin. I explained the situation and he was very understanding, if not a bit bemused.

For some reason, during lockdown, I gravitated towards reading biographies, mainly about people who have had adventurous lives and have done things that I wouldn't have done in a million years; people who have climbed ridiculously high mountains or have run a ridiculous number of marathons in a very short space of time or rowed across treacherous seas in a bathtub (OK I made that one up). If I had my time over again, I would definitely live my life more adventurously (within reason of course, no bungee jumping for me). I suppose writing this journal and sending out to publishers would be classed as being adventurous. It has definitely taken me out of my comfort zone and, instead of just reading books, I've actually written one. Maybe all that reading I did earlier on in my life helped me on a subconscious level.

Whilst writing my journal, I read *Hidden Nature A Voyage of Discovery*, written by Alys Fowler who sets out with her red inflatable kayak to explore Birmingham's hidden canal networks. I had only just started the book, when I learnt a new word; gongoozler, and it very much describes me as a gongoozler is; 'A person who enjoys watching activity on the canals' a word that just about sums me up! You never know by the time I get to the end of her book; I might be inspired to take my own kayak a bit further afield onto the Birmingham canal network, but I think I'll wait for the weather to warm up before I do.

In order to create more order and space in my book cupboard (I like a minimalist look, so all my books are in a cupboard), I filled two small suitcases with unwanted books. My original plan was to give them to a charity shop, but with all the charity shops unable to open due to lockdown, I tried a different tack and downloaded an app and, using the app I managed to sell the majority of my books. The process was easy, the company even sent a courier to collect the books free of charge. I even sold a couple of old iPhones on the site and was pleasantly surprised with the price I got for them. In case you're wondering, I donated the money from the sale of the books to charity. In addition to my books, I've also downloaded an app where I can listen to podcasts and stories, but I must admit I still prefer a good book!

It's a shame that we've lost so many independent bookshops, but I guess it proved impossible for them to compete with the online book retailers. You never know, when things go back to normal(ish) people might prefer to shop locally rather than returning to crowded shopping centres and retail parks. For me there's nothing better than browsing in a bookshop, especially if there's a coffee shop.

At the other end of the spectrum, I've never seen Phil read a book (apart from a physics textbook that is). He has no interest whatsoever in reading a book, it doesn't matter what genre it is, he's just not interested. I've tried encouraging him but to no avail, he would much rather be doing something practical than sitting down in a chair reading a book. His argument is that if he needs to read, he can use the internet.

Having written this chapter on my love of reading, I decided to do some research on *literacy* in the UK, and it seems like Phil isn't the only one who doesn't read in their free time. According to *The Reading Agency* website, "In England, 31% of adults don't read in their free time, rising to 46% of young people (aged 16 to 24)". It seems such a shame that nearly one third of the adult population are not reading in their free time. I know that lots of people were struggling over lockdown, and again, to quote *The Reading Agency*, "Reading can tackle loneliness, mental health and social mobility". Based on that information, it does sound like reading over lockdown might have helped some people, it certainly helped me.

I also looked at adult literacy rates, and according to the *Literary Trust website*, "16.4% of adults in England, or 7.1 million people, can be described as having 'very poor literacy skills.' And "...reading information from unfamiliar sources, or on unfamiliar topics, could cause problems". When it comes to young people, the result of school closures is likely to impact negatively on some of the most vulnerable and, this will no doubt leave a gap in their literacy skills. Let's hope these young people don't slip through the net and are given the time and resources to catch up with the rest of their peers

.

Happy holidays

I mentioned previously that I love to read when I'm on holiday, but did we manage to get a holiday in 2020?

It was 4th July 2020; American Independence Day, when England finally got their independence back as after weeks of restrictions, lockdown was finally relaxed and most businesses were allowed to re-open again (with the exception of hairdressers, beauty salons and gyms). It was such a relief to know that the number of deaths had decreased dramatically and, that the virus was finally on the wane (if only we'd have had a crystal ball and had seen what was going to happen a few months later). The relaxation meant that we could visit friends and family again and that in the not-too-distant future people would be able to get their hair cut for the first time in months.

With the summer stretching tantalisingly in front of us, our thoughts turned to foreign holidays. As much as we'd enjoyed being at home, the lockdown restrictions had dragged on, and the thought of going abroad and having a change of scenery was very appealing. However, at that time things were still very much up in the air as to whether or not it was safe to travel abroad. We have a holiday home in Normandy, Northern France and were anxious to get over to the house as we had a kitchen which needed to be fitted and a leaky roof which was in need of some repairs. We'd bought the kitchen units when we went over in January 2020; the units were due to be fitted in March 2020 but the lockdown both here and in France put a stop to that.

Phil and I discussed the risks and rewards of going and, after some soul-searching, we decided that the rewards far outweighed the risks. In fact, we were probably safer in France, as no sooner had the sun shown its face here in the UK, it seemed that every man, woman, and child flocked to their nearest beach; there were pictures on the news of popular beaches and beauty spots, and they were jam-packed. Heading to the nearest beach was probably not the wisest of things to do coming out of a national lockdown, but that's the great British public for you!

Phil and I have been going back and forth to France since 2006 (and I've been going for more years than I care to remember and have lots of happy memories holidaying there with my parents), which was when we bought our first. We bought a renovation project; a two-hundred-year-old stone house with a roof, windows, floors and not much else! But as soon as we saw the house, we knew it was 'the one'. However, we were very naive as we thought it would be a relatively straight forward project. In the end, it took a lot of blood sweat and tears and six years to completely renovate it. Although it took us a lot longer to complete than we'd expected (and cost a lot more), it was well worth the wait, and we had a lot of laughs along the way. Even though we sold that house, we've got some fabulous memories (and some horror stories) of those six years.

All the hard, manual work on the house was done by an ex-pat who was a friend of a friend. He was a fantastic craftsman who became a close friend of ours, but I'm sad to say that he passed away in 2017.

We always take the ferry to France, and sometimes have a cabin. However, for summer 2020, we made sure we booked a cabin for both the outward and return journeys and felt we'd done all we could to keep ourselves safe. We took a lot of food with us so that we wouldn't have to go in a supermarket too often. The ferry company was very good and, there were lots of restrictions in place in order to minimise risk. Would I have gone on holiday if I'd have had to go on a plane with over 200 other people, definitely not! Did I feel safe going to France via the ferry, I definitely did!

Once in France, the priority was to get the kitchen fitted and the repairs to the roof done, and fortunately, both jobs only took our builder friend a couple of days which meant we had another ten days left to enjoy our holiday. The weather was very hot; in fact, it's the hottest I'd ever experienced in Northern France. Keeping socially distanced in France is relatively easy unless you're in one of the big cities of course. They have roughly the same population as the UK, but the country is twice the size. Our holiday home is in a quaint medieval town with a relatively small population, so we felt very safe. One evening we met up with friends and enjoyed a wonderful three course meal in a local restaurant, it was a lovely balmy evening, and we ate 'à la plein air'. We had hoped to re-visit the restaurant we'd been to back in February 2020, but unfortunately it had closed down. Their USP of offering an intimate dining experience had actually put them out of business! The various lockdowns followed by the strict social distancing measures meant that it wasn't financially viable for them to carry on. We felt a great deal of sadness seeing the place shut up and void of customers. It's such a shame for them and all the other small businesses that have had to close, not through any fault of their own, but as a consequence of this dreadful virus.

We went to our favourite beach at Coudeville, and even though it was the height of summer, there was plenty of room on the beach. We also went to some lovely local lakes and did lots of nice walks, you can take kayaks and paddleboards onto one of the nearby lakes, so we'll pack our paddleboard next time we go. Going out and enjoying ourselves a bit too much meant that we didn't get the interior walls painted, which we'd intended to do, but that will have to wait until travel restrictions are lifted once again (which doesn't look like happening any time soon).

The French too were making the most of the post lockdown holiday season, and it was lovely to see them out with their families having picnics and BBQ's. I think the French do the best picnics; their picnics are very civilised occasions (as are most French occasions); they'll bring their own table and chairs and a tablecloth; the food always looks amazing, there's not a soggy sandwich in sight and there'll always be a bottle (or two) of wine or cider. We Brits have got a lot to learn when it comes to picnics.

Our TV wasn't set up at the time (and still isn't) so in the evenings after we'd eaten our meal or come back from a walk, Phil taught me how to play draughts. A daunting task for him, but he was up for the challenge. I think I surprised us both as I actually got quite good by the end of holiday, I even managed to beat him a couple of times (but I think he might have let me win.)

Whilst we were over there, we kept our eye on the news as it seemed that the virus was on the march again and on 26th July the UK government removed Spain from its 'safe countries' list. This meant that anyone arriving into the UK from Spain would have to self-isolate in their home for fourteen days. We were due to arrive back in the UK on 10th August and knew it would only be a matter of time before France was also removed from the 'safe countries' list. Fortunately for us, France was removed from the list on 13th August, and by that time we were safely back in the UK! For anyone who couldn't or didn't wish to self-isolate, trying to get back to the UK before the deadline date proved to be a nightmare. Prices shot up, and you couldn't get a flight or place on a ferry for love nor money.

The UK has now left the EU and travelling to other European countries will be different for me after 1st January 2021. I say things will be different for me as opposed to us, because as soon as the result of the referendum was announced in 2016, Phil saw the writing on the wall and investigated the possibility of getting an Irish passport. Fortunately for him his maternal grandfather was born in Ireland, which meant that Phil was eligible for an Irish foreign birth certificate and as a consequence an Irish passport. This meant Phil will remain an EU citizen, and he'll still have freedom of movement, free healthcare and all the other benefits which comes from being an EU citizen. I do have some Irish ancestors but unfortunately for me, they came over to the UK at the time of the potato famine, so they're too far down the family tree for me to qualify for an Irish passport. I guess I'll be at the back of the queue at passport control whilst Phil goes straight to the front — oh well, you can't win 'em all.

Not only did Phil get his holiday to France, but he also managed to get a short break to Cornwall in October. It was his friend Chris' 50th Birthday, and they'd booked a holiday cottage nine months before the pandemic hit. It was touch and go as to whether or not they'd get there as by 22nd September 2020 more restrictions had been put in place, including the closure of all pubs by 10pm; not ideal when you've got a lad's holiday planned. However, they were able to go to Cornwall the end, and they had a great time. Phil said the cottage was in an idyllic spot overlooking the beach with a couple of pubs and restaurants within easy walking distance. The weather was warm, they did some fabulous coastal walks and ate out in the local restaurants. Phil has promised to take me to Cornwall when things get back to normal and I'll hold him to that!

It's now the beginning of 2021, and as yet there's no chance of us going anywhere for the foreseeable future.

A lot of countries have closed their borders to all but essential travel and, there's now talk of having to provide a negative COVID-19 test result at all rail, air and ferry ports before returning to the UK from an overseas destination. One thing's for sure, between Brexit and COVID-19, travelling overseas won't be as straightforward as it has done in previous years.

As one door closes, another one opens

Towards the close of every year comes Christmas, and with one or two exceptions all my 2020 Christmas shopping was done online or by click and collect, and I think that's going to be the way forward for me from now on. I'd like to say that all the gifts I bought were pre-loved, but I don't think it would be fair to inflict my pre-loved penchant onto other people who may not share my vision. It's a shame for the high street stores that so many people now buy online, but the demise of the high street began before COVID-19 struck. It's just so much easier to buy at the click of a button, Phil and I even did the Christmas food shop online, so there was no need to queue up in a supermarket being jostled by people who have absolutely no concept of social distancing and/or refuse to wear a face covering. However, unlike some people we didn't put our Christmas decorations up too early: I'd never known a year when Christmas decorations went up so early, but for some families putting their decorations up early was a way for them to try and put 2020 behind them and give them something to look forward to.

There was supposed to be a relaxation of the COVID-19 restrictions over Christmas, so that families from any area of the country could meet up and spend up to five days together celebrating Christmas. However, due to the rise in the number of confirmed cases of COVID-19 and, a new more virulent strain of the virus (which is said to be a lot more transmittable than the original strain) the days we could spend with friends and family was downgraded to one day only - Christmas day! People up and down the country would no doubt have been devastated by the news that we'd been told we could only spend one day with family/friends and, a lot of money would have been wasted on food that wouldn't have been eaten. Let's hope people didn't forget that there are food banks and soup kitchens across the country that would have willingly taken any excess food

As previously mentioned, I have been a volunteer at *The Well*, a local food bank for a few years, but 2020 was busier than ever particularly over the first and subsequent lockdowns. It was busy in terms of client referrals, food donations and, busy in terms of volunteers having to work extra shifts due to colleagues having to shield. With regards to food and cash donations, it's good to know that even though people might be struggling themselves, they are still thinking of those less fortunate. Don't get me wrong, I love my work at the food bank, but in the 21st Century people shouldn't have to rely on the generosity of others; they should be paid enough either through work or by the state (where absolutely necessary) to be able to feed themselves and their family. In 2020, *The Well* fed over 11,500 people (over 7,000 adults and over 4,000 children), an increase of over 3,000 people on the previous year and, with more and more food banks opening their doors this year, it just shows how much need there is.

A recent study by the Joseph Rowntree Foundation reveals, "…an appalling rise in destitution in the UK" According to the study; "Around 2.4 million people experienced destitution in 2019, a 54% increase than in 2017. This included 550,000 children, a 52% increase since 2017, and one in seven (14%) people experiencing destitution are in paid work." If those figures weren't worrying enough, the report was published before COVID-19 so goodness knows what the next study will reveal! If nothing else let's hope all those less fortunate than us had a decent Christmas and enough food to eat. Unfortunately, the need for food banks is now greater than ever and demand shows no sign of decreasing.

We were told by the government to stay local over Christmas, and to stay at home as much as possible which we did. New Year's Eve was very low key, but the year ended on a festive note, as we a good deal of snow which lasted well into the January. Despite the freezing temperatures, we kept up our canal walks over the festive period and enjoyed them just as much as we did in the warmer weather. The frozen canals looked particularly pretty, and the tow paths and trees looked like they'd been sprinkled with icing sugar (the correct term for the icing sugar analogy is *rime*, but I thought icing sugar sounded better). We took some fabulous photographs, some of which I will use to make greetings cards, I don't know what it is, but the canals really do have a special place in my heart, whatever the weather.

So, that was 2020 and it's been interesting to say the least! Our respective families have been lucky enough not to have been affected directly by the virus and have managed to stay safe and well both physically and mentally. If I had to sum up 2020, I'd say I'd been very fortunate in lots of ways, and I'm very grateful for that. I'd also say that I've learned a lot; I've learned about virology, epidemiology and efficacy, but more importantly I've also learned a lot about myself. I'm definitely less materialistic and know whom and what is important in my life, I've learned a lot about my local area in terms of previously undiscovered nature spots that are literally on my doorstep, I've learned about new technology, I've learned how to adapt and innovate, and I've had lots of new experiences. I've even written this journal; it'll never be a best seller, but at least I gave it a go and, it will be something to reflect on in the years to come! That's what 2020 was all about for me, giving things a go and stepping out of my comfort zone. I'll admit that not everything I've tried has been a success, but at least I tried out new things and I know what I need to do in order to improve my practise.

I think everyone went into 2021 with high hopes for a bit of normality. However, hopes were dashed as by midnight on 4th January 2021, England was put into yet another lockdown (the third one) as the virus was spreading at an alarming rate as was the death rate. Once again, the government's message was for everyone to; stay at home, protect the NHS, save lives (or words to that effect; the message has changed so many times I can't keep up). Even though Phil and I have had our two vaccinations (which is great news), but it's going to be a while until the whole population has been vaccinated twice.

On a more positive note, the pandemic has shown us how resilient people can be, and we've witnessed how much good can come out of something so bad, such as the dedication of our key workers, the acts of kindness, generosity and selflessness that people have demonstrated throughout the pandemic.

It's still early days, but I can definitely see a chink of light at the end of the tunnel. You never know, by the end of 2021, things might be back on a more even keel. It has been great to see friends and family again in person without the need for a zoom call and to be able to go out to a pub or a restaurant. The lockdowns and restrictions are now but a distant memory and let's hope it stays that way. But the burning question is, will people reset their lives, and do things differently as a result of the pandemic? I would like to think they would but unfortunately, I very much doubt it! We've certainly reset ours and whatever happens, we'll try and stay positive and continue doing what we've been doing; we'll keep trying out new things and visiting new places and spaces!

EPILOGUE

It's now Autumn 2021 and, although the virus is still with us, it's definitely on the wane, helped by the fact that the vast majority of the UK adult population have had a COVID-19 vaccine. All restrictions have been lifted and life is getting back to normal, but it's still not the same as it was prior to the start of the pandemic. For example, travelling abroad can be difficult, depending on your destination and there are still a lot of people wearing face coverings, even though it is no longer mandatory to do so.

What else has changed since I finished writing my journal? Well, to start with I no longer have my car, I sold it in January 2021 and so far, I haven't missed it. I'm lucky that I'm able to use Phil's car on the occasions that I need the use of a car and I use my bike a lot more than I used to. Whether I'll want to ride my bike in the cold and wet remains to be seen! I've even kept up my resolution to only buy pre-loved clothes; in fact, I've bought very little (if anything) from that well know auction site this year and have made use of what I have hanging in my wardrobe. In fact, I can't remember when I last went clothes shopping. So far so good in terms of helping the environment.

We managed to get to France in the summer but due

to UK government bureaucracy, it proved much more difficult to get there than it did in 2020. In their wisdom, the government came up with a traffic light system for overseas travel and, when we went away in August, France was on the so-called amber list. This meant that within three days of returning to the UK we had to have evidence of a negative Covid test and in addition to that we also had to have evidence of a negative Covid test which had to be taken on day two of arriving back in the UK. This was not only time consuming to arrange but it was also costly and, for some reason, the cost of the test in the UK was more than double the price of the test that was carried out in France. Apart from blatant profiting, if anyone knows any other reason why this should be the case, please let me know. I've asked my local M.P. for an explanation, but I'm still waiting for a response.

Phil is now busier than ever and is still teaching and delivering his courses; some of which are online which means all our hard work was worth it. I'm still volunteering at *The Well,* which incidentally, was awarded the 'Queen's Award for Voluntary Service' earlier in 2021. It's good to know that all the hard work the trustees, project leaders and volunteers put in to make *The Well* the success it is today have been given the recognition they deserve.

I mentioned previously that we'd floated (pardon the pun) the idea of buying a narrow boat and, after months of research, we decided to take the plunge (apologies for another dreadful pun) and we've bought a narrow boat. We'd never even been in one, so it was something of a risk, but we just followed our hearts as it seemed like the right thing to do. Having looked at a couple of boats, we struck a deal on a 50 ft narrow boat named Mikisa. It's still early days and, the idea that we actually own a narrow boat hasn't quite sunk in (sorry, I just can't help myself with these puns)! The couple we bought her from, Alex and Pauline, were very generous, both with their time and expertise and knowing we'd never been on a narrow boat before, offered to help us get her from where she was moored nearer to where we live. We had to go through fifteen locks in total which was a real baptism of fire for our first day and the relatively short journey took us about ten hours in total. We were totally exhausted when we finally got her moored up for the night.

Phil took to the role of helmsman like a duck to water, he really is a natural. We went out on our own the following day and even though it was a tough day for us, Phil had a number of compliments on his excellent manoeuvring skills. I'm afraid I'm at the opposite end of the spectrum in terms of my skill set, and as such I've been relegated to making the tea and doing the locks. I'm sure I'll improve but it might take some time. Mikisa has now gone to a boat yard for some maintenance work and as soon as she's out, I will spruce up her interior. I won't be short of ideas as there are plenty of narrow boat forums on the various social media platforms. For the short term, she will be moored at a boat yard about five miles from our home and then, in the longer term the plan is to moor her at the bottom of our garden. However, that will be subject to permission from the *Canal and River Trust*. In the meantime, if you are thinking about doing something, my advice would be *Carpe Diem!*